I Spy

Written by
Rob Waring and **Maurice Jamall**

Before You Read

to drop something

to follow

to ride

to take something

hat

ice cream

jeans

seat

secret plans

spy

sweater

quickly

wrong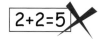

Yoon-Hee

Edgar

the woman spy

This is Edgar. Today he starts a new job. It is a very strange job. Edgar is a spy. He is in Washington D.C. in the USA. There are some papers on his table. They are secret plans. He wants to give them to a woman. She is a spy for another country. She will give him money for the plans. The phone rings. Edgar answers it.

"Hello," Edgar says.

A woman says, "Do you have the plans?" She does not say hello.

Edgar replies, "Yes, I do. Did you buy a red bag?"

"Yes. I have your money," she says. "Meet me on the White House bus at ten o'clock. I'll put the money in the red bag. Do you understand?" she asks.

"Yes," he replies.

"But I don't know you," Edgar says.

"Don't worry," she replies. "I have long black hair. I'm wearing a green sweater, blue jeans and a gray hat."

"Okay. I'll sit behind you on the bus," Edgar says. "Put your bag under your seat. I'll take your bag. Then I'll give you my red bag with the plans."

"Okay," she says. "I'll see you on the ten o'clock bus. Goodbye."

It is ten o'clock. Edgar is at the wrong bus stop. It is the Lincoln Memorial bus stop, not the White House bus stop! Edgar sees a girl there. The girl is wearing a gray hat. She has long black hair, and is wearing a green sweater and blue jeans. She is wearing the same clothes as the woman. She has the same bag, too. Her name is Yoon-Hee.

Edgar watches the girl. He thinks Yoon-Hee is the spy. He does not see the woman because he is at the wrong bus stop.

"Good, there she is. She's the woman on the phone," he thinks. "I'll get the bag and the money soon."

Yoon-Hee gets on the bus. Edgar follows her.

The woman sees Edgar with the red bag. She sees him looking at Yoon-Hee.

"Oh no," she thinks. "That's the man with the plans. He's following the wrong person. He's getting on the wrong bus!"

She runs to the bus. She wants to stop Edgar from getting on the wrong bus. But he gets on the bus. He does not see the woman.

Yoon-Hee sits down and puts her bag under her seat.

Edgar gets on the bus and sits behind Yoon-Hee.
Edgar carefully takes Yoon-Hee's red bag. He puts his bag
under her seat. Yoon-Hee now has the man's bag with the
secret papers. Edgar thinks he has the money.
"Good," he thinks. "I have the money now."
The woman is looking at Edgar. She knows Edgar has the
wrong bag!

The bus stops and Edgar gets off. He looks in Yoon-Hee's bag.
"Oh no!" he thinks. "There's no money! There's only an apple!"
The woman comes to him. "You have the wrong bag!" she says.
"I have the money here. That girl has the secret plans.
Do something!"
"Oh no!!" he says. "The bus is leaving."

Edgar sees a man on a bike. He has an idea.
He pushes the man off the bike and takes it. "Sorry!" he says.
"Hey! That's *my* bike!" says the man. "Stop!" the man shouts.
Edgar follows the bus on the man's bike. The angry man runs
after Edgar.

Edgar follows the bus. "I must get my bag back!" he thinks. He rides faster and faster and he is not riding carefully. He is not looking at the people in the park. He is only looking at the bus. Then he nearly hits a dog.

A man shouts, "Hey! My dogs! Look where you're going!"

"Sorry!" shouts Edgar. But he is only thinking about the bag. "Faster, faster!" he thinks.

Edgar does not see a woman with her ice cream.
He hits the woman and she drops her ice cream.
"Ouch!" she says. "Hey! My ice cream!"
She is angry with Edgar. "Stop! Come back!" she shouts.
But Edgar does not stop. He rides away quickly. He does
not say he is sorry.

The bus stops at the Lincoln Memorial. Yoon-Hee and her friend get off the bus.

"Good. The girl's getting off the bus. I can get the bag now," he thinks. Edgar watches her.

"Wow, this is great!" says Yoon-Hee to her friend, Kerry.

"I want to take a picture," says Kerry.

"Yoon-Hee, go over there, please," says Kerry.

Yoon-Hee puts her bag down. "Okay. Smile!" says Kerry.
Edgar sees Yoon-Hee's bag.
"There's my bag, I can get it now. I *must* get it now," he thinks.
Edgar goes behind Yoon-Hee. He does not want her to see him.
He tries to get the bag.

Suddenly, a man runs at Edgar.

"My bike," he says. "Where is it? Give me back my bike!"

Edgar is very surprised and everybody looks at them. Kerry and Yoon-Hee see Edgar. He is trying to take the bag.

Yoon-Hee takes her bag and runs to the bus.

The man says again, "Where's my bike? Give me my bike!"

Edgar is not listening. He is watching Yoon-Hee.

Yoon-Hee gets on the bus.
"Oh no!" he thinks. "She's going again!"
He pushes the man and runs to the bus, but the bus leaves.
He gets on the bike again and follows the bus.
"Hey!" says the man. "That's my bike!"

Edgar rides through the park again. He is riding faster
now. He wants his bag with the secret papers.
The woman with the ice cream sees Edgar.
She shouts at him. "Hey you! Stop!" she says.
"Give me some money for the ice cream!" she shouts.

Edgar does not listen. "Stop!" she shouts again.
The woman tries to stop him. But she cannot. The bike is too fast. She drops her ice cream again. Now she is very angry. But Edgar does not stop. He does not say he is sorry about the ice cream.
"Come back!" she shouts. But he doesn't.
She is really angry with Edgar. But Edgar is not listening. He is only thinking about Yoon-Hee and his bag.

Edgar follows the bus through the park. He does not see the man with the dogs.
"Hey! It's you again!" says the man.
The bike nearly hits the dogs again. But Edgar does not stop and he does not say he is sorry. He rides away.
The man is very angry.

The bus stops at the museum. Edgar sees Yoon-Hee and Kerry get off the bus. Edgar gets off the bike. He watches Yoon-Hee go into the museum.
"Oh no! She's going into the museum! She has the secret papers," he thinks.
"What can I do? I must get the papers! I must stop her!"

Edgar runs at Yoon-Hee and tries to take the bag.

"That's my bag," says Edgar.

"No, it's *my* bag!" shouts Yoon-Hee. They are both pulling on the bag.

Kerry helps Yoon-Hee. "Hey! Hey! That's mine!" says Yoon-Hee.

"No, it's mine," says Edgar. "Give it back to me!"

Edgar and Yoon-Hee pull on the bag. The bag breaks and the secret papers go everywhere.

Suddenly, the men, the woman, and the dogs all arrive. They are all very angry with Edgar.

"He took my bike," says a man.

"Look at my dress! He did that!" says the woman.

The other man says, "He hit my dogs!"

"Get him!" they all shout and they all jump on Edgar.

Yoon-Hee looks at some of the papers.

"Look at this!" says Yoon-Hee. "These are secret papers."

"Let's tell the police!" says Kerry.

The police officers come. They take Edgar to the police station.

"Oh no!" thinks Edgar. "And this is my first day in my new job!"